The Frame Called Ruin

Hadara Bar-Nadav

New Issues Poetry & Prose

A Green Rose Book

New Issues Poetry & Prose
The College of Arts and Sciences
Western Michigan University
Kalamazoo, Michigan 49008

Printed in the United States of America.

First Edition, 2012.

ISBN: 978-1-936970-08-7 (paperbound)

Library of Congress Cataloging-in-Publication Data:
Bar-Nadav, Hadara.
The Frame Called Ruin/Hadara Bar-Nadav
Library of Congress Control Number: 2011943423

Editor:	William Olsen
Guest Editor:	Nancy Eimers
Managing Editor:	Kimberly Kolbe
Layout Editor:	Elizabyth A. Hiscox
Assitant Editor:	Traci Brimhall
Art Director:	Paul Sizer
Designer:	Zachary Ruden
Production:	Paul Sizer The Design Center, Frostic School of Art College of Fine Arts Western Michigan University
Printing:	McNaughton & Gunn, Inc.

The Frame Called Ruin

Hadara Bar-Nadav

New Issues
WESTERN MICHIGAN UNIVERSITY

The Frame Called Ruin

Also by Hadara Bar-Nadav

A Glass of Milk to Kiss Goodnight
Show Me Yours

To my family here, abroad, and beyond

Contents

A space must be maintained or desire ends.

—Anne Carson

And you are a rare modern painting in the grand salon
And you are a wall of earth.

—Lisa Robertson

I.

Write Paris out of the Pictures

Tel Aviv's face wears a makeup
of ash. Dust climbs
cheekbone to eyelash.

In the open face of light
women hide like spiders in a well
(*I am not well, I am not well*).

Here comes the junk man
with his little cart
and horse skeleton.

The apartment floods
with dreams—*how much*
for the wedding ring?

Trade a necklace of bullet shells
while the windows rain.
A suicide of buildings.

The landscape blushes,
redly bruised. Hair
unraveling at the root.

Alleys collect finger bones,
calicos and crying.
A soldier touches my crying,

my sun-freckled breasts.
Drink and the wine
licks our bruised lips.

We cannot go to the movies.
Streets empty, close.
We race to where the city

ends. The beach is riddled,
waters bleed. Days
crumble unceremoniously.

Alarm Pleasures into Hum

Mutiny awakens me,
the kingdom buzzing with saws,
all the fetishes abloom

which means a rubbing away until
blood or speech, each
to his own bright unraveling.

Red lives here, a nest
of nerves and twigs.
Doors unhinge and the roof

speckled with stars:
holes, navels, scars.

I have no floor,
no caviar, no mints.

I am humble as a tooth
and hunger.

And you are the messenger
without bell or tongue.

You are the messenger.

Come.

Structures of a Softer Sort

Here's a plain pile of sand.
    Watch it tall
    and mount itself.

A window gives birth
    to a thousand windows.
    Makes a tin and eggy sound.

Scent. Sunlight snakes
    along an elevator shaft.
    Weightless with yellow heft.

Add white and cook
    on a fire-resistant spoon
    until ceilings fry fluorescent.

Make a picnic with pinkish
    ham. Or we are the picnic—
    your kittenish cheek and laugh.

Demure buildings desire
    control. A study of winged backs
    and collarbones. Immured

by patterns, the dance called flow.
    Scaffold when the sky falls.
    And it does. Your chin

lightly fuzzed like a doe's.
    In the forest of my unmaking
    the cubicles are full

of holes. What shaky walls.
    Aren't we all? Bones
    no longer ballast.

Each of us a trembling mirror
    of I of you of him of her
    skinned in glass.

Blur

After the bombs
and the buildings blow
I call Clover, Clover
and you appear—
a dream limned in smoke.

Clover, my hermaphroditic dear,
I kiss your singed
leaflet ears and fawn
in a café in Eilat.
Clover sips from a demitasse.

Only a few sesame seeds left
and the porcelain carried away.
Morning crawls toward
afternoon and the sun
says it's time for wine

to drown this red day.
I hear there's a crater
where our bed last lay
at the Hotel de Ruin.
A portrait of dancing

lights and fire balloons,
a painterly gasoline blur.
Let's find a sailboat,
bread, za'atar, and figs
and watch the distance burn.

Crystal Palace

Desire predates the invention of glass.
The eyes will travel. And the light.

Your mouth cathedrals.
Your hand, a golden cup.

We all glisten in the conservatory.
The sun circles and pools.

Vaulted halls and a million feet of shine.
All those zeros. Openings into the woods.

My jacquard loom, my envelope machine.
Translucence drowns the eyes.

There is room inside. Many rooms.
Glass groom, glass bride.

Lust and Smoke

You overwhelm me with your dress
always lifting, always falling.
Velvet parting, velvet portiere,
many callers (lifting, falling).

Many admirers admire
your velvet hallways and the silk
faux-Victorian settee
ribboned in scarlet and smoke.

How to compete with a tent so big?

Your dress hung from a tree,
your dress waving from a tower
and then your dress breathtaking on TV,
the reporter bleeding from her mouth.

All the people line up to see you
radiant in firelight, with shreds
of cotton in their fists
and their fists in their mouths.

The smoke is thick inside this tent.
And you, volcanic, spread.
Velvet ash, velvet wish.
Soon we are crawling. We are dead.

Let Me Hold the Kaleidoscope

So the sun splits and
    splits us again.

So the angles knife the bakery
    and butcher shop, and the poodle
    has three heads.

One blue touches another
    but refuses to match
    (cobalt, phthalo, bruise).

The telephone wires never touch
    themselves, not even at night
    when the lips are asleep.

What jagged teeth you have
    dotting your flushed cheeks
    and the arrows of your burnt hair.

Take me to the door with six peepholes.
    Take me up the impossible stairs,
    an accordion of torsion and thrust.

Everything unbuttons and we
    forget about war,
    its itchy apparatus.

Romance nevertheless is true,
    the moon a cluster of shredded sequins,
    deconstruction a song for two.

To see you clearly
    in all of your parts—
    the slip of your earlobe and sigh.

Icarus in Love

Beholden to the woman with the most redolent *Ls*
I dreamt of the cello of her back.

Charlotte thrummed by a man's hands,
then rising above the monument.
Her waist tied to a hundred balloons.

Shapely nude with shapely folds.
Curls, vulva, ankles.

*

My tongue grew the length of a spine
turning child to fish to child.

Tongue jutting forward for *leap, little, lick*.
A space between front teeth where I split
my mouth, the skin badly stitched.

*

Asterisk, navel, stars in my eyes.
A woman flies without wings!

*

Charlotte, I love you in the sky.
Lithe. Lift.

Our ample mouths and intermingling myths.
Your hips, my sky. My wrist, your plinth.

To Halve and to Hole

At three a.m. when I'm glass again
millions of little red chairs dangle
like marionettes, twinkle

like teeth. So they don't flatten my head I wish
for a black hat. I wish for one black hat
and then more.

I am jealous of men with black hats.
How fine it must feel
to be cupped.

At dawn the glass is full of pleases,
orange mixed with pink and the sun
bleeds out.

I sit in a red chair festooned with light
and wooden pleading, catch teeth
in my hat and bleed out.

> Look, we're all in roses now.
> Look, the eyes gone like a surprise
> and a soft fur in the holes.

We used to be so spiny, red fretworks
of shadow and bone. How beauty suggests
beau geste and the ribs part

themselves for breath. Then the great
unraveling, a spool of blood
and bread.

Remember the blue feather and
leather circlet, boiled wool shaped
to your form?

What's holding us up anymore?
Close my eyes,
try to recall.

Night, White, and Gold (for Louise Nevelson)

I. *Sky Cathedral*

Shadow is my paint, the inky blue-black of it, shifty the way sunlight strikes and disintegrates. No light in the deep. My forest of black boxes. My milk box and lettuce crate. 38 boxes stacked high and wide. Each box, a theater in black. Diorama with shapes turning inside: a wooden duck, hatter's block, chair rail, ten pin. My empire dipped in matte black paint. My gothic rise without end or tip.

If I were a man would you call it "dollhouse?" Tracery, finery, and lace? A wall has certain mass and weight. Focus on forms and vacancies. I own my voids, deepest black. And now my secret is out: I'm motherhouse. My son in Maine while I studied art with strange men in Germany. And that isn't all. I told the boys in The Club I had balls. Oh, draw your damn curtains, you won't block me out. I've made you a toppling dollhouse. My high wall of boxes just for you. Are you my child? May I bathe you in flood? A wall can tidal, light disintegrate. Cathedral means holy and scrape. I could tear the sky, and the waters break.

II. *Dawn's Wedding Feast*

Begin at the edge of skin. Where are you in the landscape? *This fan with beautiful ribs.* Black into gold. Now white. Dimension counts on its fingers: 1, 2, 3, 4, and I make my shadows light. Even white has her shadow. Dawn, her silver fan. In *Dawn's Wedding Feast* forms are being wed. Table top to leg, porch post to bed. My first white, first flat girl-bride, forms and thighs laid on the table. Able, bounty, feast. The landscape unveils a wedding suite. You be the day and I'll be the night, hand in hand in white.

Assemble for the feast. Assembly of pieces and the pieces assemble into shapes. The feast, a landscape of skin that begins with cake, a pillow, chapel, and baluster case. And then there's the mirror where we meet. Enter and eat. Pause and sweeten, cheek to cheek. The body is meat. Call me lambchop, honey, or Louise. Please pass the landscape. Gravy of tears and white paint. I'll never again marry, but the cities we'll build, the shadows we'll shape. White landscape where we forsake our names, undone by the love of making.

III. *Dreamhouse*

I wanted a house. Bi-level. Split. A house to house me, feed me with. Wood the color of gingerbread burned sweet. Licorice walls, black forest bricks. Frosting shaped into plump hens and pigs. Raisin bread in the oven, butter slit. 30th street, my apartment in parts. Make use of each discarded piece. Toy chest and cherry-wood heart. I'd marry a house, sing songs, gather wood. We'd wed each day, woman and room. House who waits with longing kisses and stares. House who longs for me: body, box, oval, square.

Architect of shadows and shapes. Dream a dreamhouse, dreambox filled with people. Sweet filling like cake. Swilling with people, a boisterous lot. House of cozy, besotted, and cot. A fluted bed for a boy who dreams in Maine. A lovely space for people and shapes. House filled with finials, rectangles, chairs. Dozens of chairs for shapes to sit, for shapes to chat, liquor, and cake. Miles away with shadows and shapes, I wait for you in lovely space.

IV. *The New Continent*

Couldn't keep it whole. Total. Nobody would have it. *I've destroyed so much.* Even *Dawn's Wedding Feast.* I would have given it away, but instead reassembled the pieces. *The New Continent*, another forest in black. That's what I do. Lay the names down in shadow. Present in shadow. Disappear in light. When everything is black, safety among objects. I take them from your bedrooms, kitchens, bars, schools, and will not name them banister or child. I love them all. I make a wall and build them each a room.

Look at time and it passes. I left time, a boy who dreams in Maine, a husband, Kiev when I was three, the names and shapes of things. The dark makes us present, equivalent. Even *Self-Portrait* in tattistone is black. Black is *Relief.* Safety in shadows. Anonymity of shapes. Table leg and armchair finally released. Difficult ornaments from someone else's dream. Regret swallowed with memory.

V. *Assemblage with Night*

I'll make room for you in my bed. Bed of maple, oak, ash, or my sweet favorite cherry. I kneeled in the dust, smelled it on his clothes. My father owned a lumberyard, which means wood was home. Familiar, though I plunged each piece into paint—black, white, and gold—to unhinge the familiar, anonymously at home. Later there was aluminum and steel. Whole monuments storeys and stories high. High stories, stacking one story on another. Each box with letters inside. I turned to Lucite, epoxy, and glass to be closer to the light. I wore silver armor around my neck and walked through the day thinner than light. Darling, I was disappearing. Wind passed through the thin room of me. A tumor inside the room of my mind. So light and thin I could feel my skull lifting at the seams. At last my mind released me. The boxes watched.

A wall full of stories. A wall like a letterpress, like letters being set. Leading like leather and setting. Kerning like kernel and keening. A wall to lean on, simple as hope. *Either you would stay there or cut your throat.* Such mercy inside shadow and form. Each box, a loving alphabet of its own. Each wall, an assembly of letters left behind. Discarded, I found them on the streets at night.

Look at time and it passes. Like a twitch. In the end, even fabric and paper were knit. The pieces, ready-made and willing to hinge. Assemblage, montage, collage, architectural debris, detritus, free, found on the street, offal, piecemeal, a meal in pieces but a meal nevertheless. Piecing is feminine. I saved each piece to hinge and knit. I gathered each and myself into the landscape. Salvaged a doorknob and a day.

II.

Still Life (with Death)

We were burned, and we were blind.
  We wanted to record the occasion of us,
  so stole sheets from a sagging clothesline
  and wrapped them around our heads.

This is decoration—inhaling damp heat
  through the rose-colored gauze
  of our bandaged faces.

Every shadow loved me, every eyeless
  girl made of cunning and wind.

We owned nothing but ourselves
  and we were only an idea.

In a church parking lot I found a man's
  tweed suit and a box of pastels
  the color of a bakery and drew you
  shoulders, a dress, and pink shoes.

Our heads full of flies and violins, we tucked
  and smoothed our new skins and sat
  for our portrait on a Sunday afternoon.

We scared away the half-drunk picnickers and raised
  their cheese sandwiches in the air.

The hours stood still. Even the worms
  held their breath.

My Wife in All Things

My wife the sun. A chiffon dress lit with poppies and devilish hearts. Buttershine on a dinner roll for a dinner I missed. Her mouth salty butterscotch.

My wife the starlings. Their dust-black feathers and mouse-small faces stitched with stars. Skeletal legs threaded dark pink and jagged hopping that looks like joy.

My wife birch trees. The uranium factory near our apartment encircled by trees. Ash peeled to ash. Slender kneeling in the wind. A lace of burned fingers.

Wife hours, wife sleep. We dragged our mattress to the rooftop where the breeze was always night. Children quiet as ash. No light could be heard fanning among us, but the sirens circled our glass-dark heads.

Wife flesh, tender palace of the ears, tender net between shoulder and neck. A necklace of blood. Explosions overhead and the eardrums blow. She feels where blood falls and touches it. A red sound and its hammer.

Wife ribbon, knife, apple skin. She stayed red for months, hidden in my pocket until she puckered, a brown sack. I was the only one with a wife, an apple. My precious red love. This secret made me smile, even as the city wept.

Wife bodies laid out in rows with their eyes still open. Each one (not) my wife, wrapped in strips of white cloth. Her black moviestar eyes watch from the street, the newspaper, the television. Alive. Alive again, all the eyes hers.

The Women Are Naked Again

Women are devoured by lobsters or bees
dancing all the while.

Plunder of surly lovers
surely licking popsicle lips.

Naked in the city, in the mosque, on a pirate ship,
missing their feet or wearing cotton candy heels,
clutching an axe or another woman's squeal.

A day at the beach holding a yellow balloon.
Thread bikinis in pinks, reds, and blues.

Women pregnant with deer and doom.
Fragrant with dear and roses, how are you?

Fire ants like a good eyepatch and melted face.
Fester another word for fine weather,
a fine day or fair-weather friend.

Let's get naked and dirty in daylight!

*

Platform shoes go great with church.
Do you like my hair on fire?

I like you naked with Nordic braids,
I like your sandy bones.

Let's climb a tree and hang you
upside down by your knees
while bears eat your honeyed mouth.

Let's go for a swim and curdle,
the sun an oily streak.

Let's roast our faces like marshmallows.
and burn each other's panties.

Naked and dirty in daylight!

*

Half woman half bear half deer half naked half loving half
dead woman on stilts woman deboned woman wearing
a woman wearing salty vinyl and skin wearing teeth
wearing saws and red-nailed feet wearing beehives
petroleum and wax candy lips wearing neon eyes
violet boots gas masks and cactus bathing suits

*

I have a wish and a city inside.
Open my _____ and look.

Unité d'Habitation

I have decided to make beauty by contrast.
—Le Corbusier

It was an ugly time. Streets in the sky
as close as we would get. We kept
losing the door. Without a place to enter
no one left. Even the fire escape could kill you.
After the war 1,600 of us lived in a vertical
village slab without enough steel to hold us in.
La Maison du Fada, a form of insanity, inspired
a plague of ideas. How frightening
the giant turtle and nursery on the roof,
the bulbous barbershop and ironic hotel
with its many chins. The balconies jutting,
avuncular mustaches you'd refuse to kiss.
Gardens edged with moldy skirts, unending
fields of green. Instead of confetti, concrete.
An epidemic that spawned twelve stories
and infected Nantes, Firminy, and Berlin.

Be My Plate

Sometimes I want a corset

        to harden me or garnish,

to flail against the edges,

        centrifuge of blood

and dangling heat

        (heart in my teeth).

Corset for thought

        chattering (be still,

my teeth). Sometimes

        a garnish and come-hither

gesture, but parsley,

        just for taste, a pretty

necessity that in turn

        holds up vertebrae,

the way you sew

        yourself: dimple, whale

bone, 52 difficult eyes,

        and an electrical cord

coursing the length

        of a system skirted

in eyeleted lace.

My soft illusion

of barely held stays,

rapt by invitation,

prettily contained.

Fields, Ribbons, Folds: Somatic Landscapes (for Zaha Hadid)

(Adapted from Zaha Hadid's project notes)

I. *The Centre of the Body*

The circulation system is a three-dimensional jigsaw puzzle made up of solids and voids running the full length of the lobby. A three-dimensional jigsaw puzzle curves slowly upward as it enters, running the full length of the body. Pedestrian movement curves slowly upward as it enters the dynamic public space. Pedestrian movement forms an undulating translucent skin. The dynamic public space forms a series of polished surfaces covered in undulating translucent skin. Passers-by see into the life of the Centre through a series of polished surfaces. Passers-by are the light of the Centre, a circulation system made of solids, voids.

II. *Vitra's Dance*

As one passes through the fire station
        one catches glimpses of fire engines,
                a series of choreographic notations.
        Their lines of movement inscribe the asphalt.

One catches glimpses of fire engines.
        Similarly, firemen will be inscribed into the ground.
                Their lines of movement inscribe the asphalt
        which punctures, tilts, and breaks.

Firemen will be inscribed into the ground,
        defining space rather than occupying space
                which punctures, tilts, and breaks.
        Walls appear to slide past each other

defining space rather than occupying space.
        Like the lines of light
                walls slide past each other
        with precise and fast movement.

Like the lines of light
        one passes through the fire station.
                The precise and fast movement
        like a series of choreographic notations.

III. *Operatic Space*

You can eliminate wasted space by very simple moves,
    in terms of planes, in terms of spatial organization.

By very simple moves my work began to be about volumes
    and spatial organization. The project became projected space.

My work began to be about volumes, about layers of volumes
    becoming projected space as opposed to layers of planes.

These layers of volumes are like reading the Bible
    as opposed to layers of planes. You have to be able to move

around them like reading the Bible or any set of religious guides.
    You have to be able to move around them so that buildings

can allow air and light. Like any set of religious guides
    these things are fluid, not rigid. Even buildings can allow

air and light. Through precision and interpretation
    you can eliminate wasted space. Through precision

and interpretation, even buildings become fluid.

IV. *Soon, the Garden*

Interwoven spaces are caught. One path snuggles up to the south side. Another, gently sloping, rises over its back. The third cuts diagonally through the interior. One path snuggles up to the south side. The surrounding network of paths cuts diagonally through the interior and entangles to make the building. The surrounding network of paths half submerged in the ground entangles to make the building, which emerges from the fluid geometry. Half submerged in the ground, the root of the building emerges from fluid geometry. The space for the garden festival roots the building. In the space for the garden festival, interwoven paths are caught, gently sloping, rising toward each other.

The Sun Also Lonely

When I drink milk less lonely

When I hear the upstairs neighbor walk across my bed less lonely

Or take a shower in unison with him less lonely

And keep the nightlight on though I'm well past childhood

Though I have an encyclopedia and a globe

And stash KY Jelly in my nightstand

And have chapped lips from kissing the back of my hand

Though I fall in love with a good nut-bread

Though I have a picture of a woman on a keychain

Though she's smaller than a thumbprint and already dead

Though I sometimes share my bed with a poodle less lonely

And convince myself less lonely

That ultra-white teeth and wrinkle cream less lonely

And strip my bikini line less lonely

And stand too close to strangers on the elevator

And go to a tailor who touches my breasts

Though I eat breakfast with the television

And have a limitless cellular plan

And never pretend I'm talking to someone on the phone less lonely

Or listen to my earbones crack

Or chew the insides of my cheeks

Or hear my neighbor hum during sex with someone less lonely

Or wait less lonely for the sun to break

Abandoned Dome

I leaked.

And my ceilings went on forever.
　　You could lose your head and kite.
　　You could fall in love with distance
　　and grow lonely at the same time.

I could never be divided.
　　I wanted you wholly.
　　I wanted to lick your open spaces, your paranoia,
　　the damp salt behind each knee.

Come, let me charm you in my whisper gallery
　　where I can hear you breathe from the other side of the moon
　　and when you moan, each window moans too.

My sounds once delighted—
　　triangle, pentagon, icosahedron, ding-dong, I miss you.

The front door, so difficult to open, meant *please* and *stay*,
　　love insulating this private balloon.

III.

Severance

Tore my waist from my hips
and floated above myself.

Helium bust
in a world full of pins.

Let go of friction,
ruffles, rubber, sweat.

Severance
is such sweet sorrow.

The heavy half below
unraveling, sick

as mud, mud legs,
mud bowels, and bath

while the kite of me
blotted out the sun.

Would my legs forgive me,
beg for my return?

And had I been kind?
Enough hot air to last for miles.

In the meantime, my waist scabbed
a pale gray-green

and the navel would reject me,
little key

that I had once belonged
to the suckling world.

And I wished to cover myself,
wished for the waistcoat

with cherry buttons
I had loved as a child

when grief was a girl
and pocket small,

not this Hindenburg heart,
a hemorrhaging clot

scaring away the spectators
and sinking.

Two-Inch Figure Standing on an Inkwell

Mother carries a gun in one hand,
a feather in the other. Mother,
large as a swollen thumb.

Southern belle in gauzy skirts
and pantaloons, through linen and sun,
her ankles and calves.

Skin like paper, paper like skin
whipped thin. The horizon rises
behind her, a landscape of serifs and wind.

The sky turns funnel and green.
All the animals silent. The flight
of fathers and firetrucks,

feathers but no birds calling.
Our house surrenders its walls and roof:
lath, thatch, thumbtacks, and glue.

A notebook spine makes a rickety ladder.
The sky is falling. Flooding.
Safety and escape are long gone

abstractions from childhood.
Mother pulls the trigger and spirals.
Her feet ink the snow.

The Flood Comes and the Basement Floats

The frightening egg sacks
are frightening I tell you. The size
of baby teeth grown soft with rot.

Bubbling cotton sacks beating
from the inside. Sacks full of muffled
mouths, muffled legs. Clot.

I make us a paper boat. Get in
children, husband, and dog. I steer us
around the basement and play

keep-away from the drain, a whirlwind
in the corner by the washing machine.
A concrete dimple like a smile awaits.

What we see: the top of murky windows.
Some grass. The piqued ears of rabbits
who will eat us with their sweet

furry faces and cute teeth. I paddle fast
with my popsicle-stick arms. We have
so little our dreams become bread.

Now nightmares will save us. O death
in black, in silvery lead, what a relief
you are with your charcoal-crusted hands.

The unborn drag beneath us, lint
clinging to our perforated edge.
Egg sacks on which I lay my head.

Shall we visit the wool sweaters?
The used checkbooks, boxes
marked Void and Void?

Or the ashes of a war, a family?
The wilting photographs
and their blurry gray milk?

Perhaps the mattress will save us, a rectangle
of a whale made of memory foam
freckled with suspicious mold.

But she floats. Everybody off!
Leave your life vests
on the lines. An invitation

to a salty, sweaty sleep. Transfer
your belongings from one sinking
to another. You must have hope

even though you have no belongings.
You must have hope to ride
the girl of your dreams.

Carriage Abandoned at the Beach

For years I pretend to be a gate
between gravity and sleep.

My silver handle for hands to push,
handle for hands (to release).

Polyester-caped frame and rubber wheels.
Clavicle for cloth and skin.

Now fog rots the fabled spokes
where I once thought a god lived.

Stranded, I bear down, sink in the sand,
nautilus netting what I can.

Inside me gather the small, round backs
of shells with no sounds inside.

My whites crust to yellow,
my silver peels to rust.

The tide salts the wreckage
and recedes.

The foam and crest like milk except
for the acidic suck and seethe.

Bricolage and Blood

I'm stuck here in the abattoir,
a fancy word for *eat my fatted heart.*

I've been a cow before
two lives ago and a woman
who gave too much in between.

It's all tautology, a cyclic chewing
on the same bit.

Call it cud—in this life
my tongue mixed with grass
and in the previous, Chivas with tears.

I've been patient.
I've been given something to do
and I've done it phatically.

So much noisier a life ago when I choked
and died in a strange man's bed.

> I had seen death in his face,
> the beautiful skull
> articulated beneath his skin.

I wish I were in my last life, or my first.
But for now I'm dying again
(a redundancy in red).

The familiar passage
smells like blood.

Four Reds (for Rothko)

I. *Colorwheel*

Mix cinnabar and ochre with eggs. Then light. Where to go once red lunges into fire? *My servile edges aflame* sounds as if an end is redly near. How quickly the chemical swallows and peels: saffron, vermilion, cadmium blue tipped with teeth. Very meditative. Also agitative. Fire spins its colorwheel. Prayerwheel. Sequels of fur-lined syntax melt. The flame, a triangle with eyes at the apex and silvery feet. The body, a matchstick house. A house is always burning, breathing commonly hard. I'm advised by specialists to arrange an elaborate fish tank and comfortable leather chair. Watch every day how slowly life moves in Anotherland. Add salt and flakes. Watch every day how slowly life eats. And so full of color.

II. *Paper Conversion*

There was red and then there was red. *Red and Pink on Pink*, *Three Reds White Cloud* (which is red), *Brown and Black in Reds*, and even just *Red*, though in the end *Black on Gray*. Several of them. There had been *Green and Tangerine on Red* and *Ochre and Red on Red*. *Black on Dark Maroon*. Yes. I could work with some pills, some pills but not others, and then a flood of paper with paint and my heart still swollen sick but yes, there were paintings. Hundreds flying from my hands. You could see the progression. Dvinsk, Russia to Oregon and then New York. My final resting place, East 69th Street.

In the end I had to work on paper. Like some writer. It was my heart, an aneurysm of the aorta and no more canvas, canvas, canvas had held me for so long. And then paper. Roll after roll of slick surface. No teeth. Paper, like some goddamn writer, but no pen, no pencil, no keys. Dumb heart. Dumb paintbrush. Then it was mostly brown or black on gray and a skinny white border that bobbled. A skinny white seam for red to break.

III. *The Art of Untitled*

A period says when to begin or end but who really knows. I spend hours and days inside red trying to solve syntax. Savage. Salve. Save. My hands big as horses, as houses. Big as buildings. Does somebody have a cigarette and light? Scale has gone and the cigarettes return proportion. The size of red? Distortion. To make a sentence impossible now. No more titles or names. No more *red*.

To float one layer on top of another. How to be perfectly still. Perfectly flat yet layer one on the other. For example, *Four Darks In Red*, *Horizontal White Over Darks*, or *Untitled (Brown and Gray)*, or *Untitled* and *Untitled* and *Untitled*. And then they wanted me to make a church, and I did. A chapel, and everything went dark.

Marcus Rothkowitz is not my name. Never trust language and words will unglue. The flatness of the picture plane. Purity of pigment. Purely flat. Never trust a name. *Untitled* and *Untitled*. Direct experience and exchange. It's all very mathematical. Very spiritual. I'm not even here. Here the paintings are made by no one. *Untitled* and *Untitled*.

IV. *Black, Maroons, and White*

Look how red can eat in *Brown and Black in Reds* and *Four Reds.* Hungry Little Red Riding Red. Red forest. Red clouds. Clouds over a red lake. A grandmother and a wolf. I made a brick house in *Black, Maroons and White.* A bole chimney and uneaten loaves of bread. A cherry pie with forked crust and secret slivers of lemon peel. The mooncloud of God dissolves, foaming at the wolf's mouth. Sticky liver. Lover. Sliver. To eat a woman's mouth, tie her lace and cotton bonnet underchin. My chin. Trick or treat. Or meat. My little inamorata, my lithe little pumping red. I wait for you with God on my side. Who eats, lives.

Dim the light and darken the hues. A parachute taped to the skylight so I can see the pigment glow, a hidden light source only the pigment knows. *The spirit and space, the empty spirit in vacant space.* Shallows of color swallow others. The wine-red sea opens to drown me. Only the wolfish pigment knows where the red ends and black begins, where black rises over red and red recedes against maroon, where black washes into green and green breaks in two and red is vanquished and swallows us like pearls.

Construction

I teeter at the edge of the air well.
    They've ripped out the elevators
    and now 110 stories open up—
    an invitation of invisible arms
    pulling downward.

I drop my cigarette, watch it arc,
    a white finger penetrating the dark
    until the dark lashes out, swallows.

The smallest sounds carry.
    I clear my throat and it comes
    back to me three times.

I yell my name, then my lover's,
    and the names of those who've died.
    The names hook their hands
    around my ears.

Astragal

n. anklebone; rounded beading or molding on a column;
n. divination by anklebones or dice.

The divine beads
of the anklebones

decorate a door
with clatter and chink.

Phantom feet make
pleasant chimes.

If you can no longer walk,
wind.

If you are dead do you need
such decoration?

What once touched
ground, severed, strung.

Imagine the column—
legs suddenly strange,

a stranger's body caught mid
breath, the step kicked out,

the dangling music of
Nancy, of Avram.

Ache Becomes "Embankment"

You're not still casting the insides of things, are you?
—Question asked of Rachel Whiteread
in response to her sculpture *Embankment*

To see a thing whitely with edge
pour concrete, plaster, polyethylene.

Yes, a cast water bottle.
Yes, a staircase and a chair.

Yes, the space underneath the bed where I was born
and a Victorian living room that reminded me of home.

Yes, a condemned house in London (later bulldozed),
and a library in Vienna (lined with six million ghosts).

I used to seal the bodies *in*,
affix the lids of coffins.

Now inside becomes out and the light
is arctic.

A shape and the shape that surrounds it (glint),
the shape negative space leaves behind.

—inside, over, outside, behind, between, beside, underneath—

After she died, I cast a cardboard box
filled with toys my mother saved.

14,000 ways to contain loss.
14,000 containers arranged.

Mother of a maze piling skyward.
Our empire of ghosts.

Monument a word with a woman inside
(or a woman outside in the dirt).

Absence files in pressing me
to the walls, to the roof.

A complete emptiness the exact size
of a room.

IV.

Fable of Flesh

At 4 a.m. the bells
        swallow their song
    and a spine swings in its cage.

If a woman is a dream,
        what the spine dreams of,
    warm balcony at the top of the tongue,

how many rooms does she bring?
        Stories hung about her neck
    and waist like the iron weight

of a dowry. Hair tightly pulled
        and a burlap dress, nevertheless
    toothsome in shadows, statuesque.

The temple pauses on one foot
        to listen to the deep between
    breaths. Who knew a world

of crutches and stilts awaits,
        a tilt just above sinking?
    The palace hears branches

canticle in winter, the palace
        longs for Avignon in spring.
    The splintered aftermath—

an abstract of wood, wire,
        string, and a pair of wings
    stretched and pinned

to the walls. Here we are flightless
        but we are not alone, here
    we are so thin.

Meet Me (Breathless)

on the corner of sky and lamppost. I will look for you so wear your eyes. Wear your face that has slept in curls. I will breathe the tulip scent of your hair and the sidewalk's soot-lined snow. Don't forget to bring your delicate feet, those edible toes uncold in your oversized men's boots. I will come with my hands holding bread—broad loaves creased with rosemary. And I will come with wine, two plummy reds bearing bicycles, top hats, and names we cannot pronounce. Bring your accordion mouth and your love of emptiness. Bring a fire and the wild nest of your neck. Bring your open throat.

I Used to Be Snow White

                    but I drifted
and the seven small men
who set up video cameras left.

My 13-inch face floats
inside the television like soap
bobbing on a bathtub's wave.

You prop me on the edge
of your dresser, splay
my antennae to spear the stars.

I dance until your satellites
blow, the static buzz
exchanged for romance.

Thank you for the candle
and ashtray though I've no
fingers, no cigarettes.

Also, I'm cut off below
the neck (O, the things
I'd do if I had hands).

Still, I feel so close to you.
Whistle to me across
this expanse.

Crash and Burn

The basement drops first, too heavy
        to lift. Goodbye mortar and stone
with a penchant for mold. Goodbye
        grandfather clock with your broken
gong and a piano missing half its teeth.
        Boxes of books and baby clothes
shock from sudden light. Spiders cleave
        to every fold, their hairline mouths
and sticky sacks shatter in a shower
        of concrete. The living room refuses
to land, a triangular cape with shingled
        wings that cries from Calgary to Cancun
and back again, smashing windows along
        the way, ripping free of the chimney's
brick and drag. Wires unravel
        like veins across the sky, dance
a secret alphabet. Vertigo for the TV
        and stereo who bury themselves at sea.
The bedroom surrenders ivory walls, splayed

open, vulnerable without curtains.

The queen bed slumps her bulk against

an oak. Crows shred her ticking heart.

Inside the Maze (I)

In springtime, my lush season to feed, I never even try to leave. Berries (reds and deep blues) line the maze plentiful and nipple sweet. A sugar-crusted path of days opens up before me. Dulcet corridors of decay. Pleasure caked in rot. Afternoons I laze in the honeyfull sun and scrape my teeth with a virgin's thumb.

Inside the Maze (II)

Of course I knew the maze better than any maiden or youth. At most they had three days while I sharpened and shined my horns on the bones and fat of their siblings. They all begged *Quick, Quick*, and I did because once my tips were inserted I couldn't forgive (red every inch). I could ram the walls and tunnel through but where would I live? *Exile.* And why leave? *Pariah. Derelict.* My palatable palace. My difficult plate. Here I am sated. Sate me.

Inside the Maze (III)

Mother: woman. Father: bull and here I am cut at the middle part fraction with a line below the navel part collision of horns and feet. I know the word for monster. I also know I am the sun of a queen and a divine white bull I'll never see, though perhaps in their way they love me. Every nine years they send me fourteen children to eat. *They feed me*. They multiply their fractions, sever their lines, while the kingdom rages. The kingdom divides. Once I watched two half-breeds, a boy and a man fly above my maze, one whose yarrow scent I recognized as the maker of my walls. I prayed to the gods that he alone should know my pain and watched his winged boy fall.

Inside the Maze (IV)

Starlings clean me, peck mites and fleas from my fur and yawn inside my ears. The black flapping I wear like a second skin. I've pulled arrows from their dead. They've been hated longer than me and we both live in the leaves, a green called home. My fragrant catalogue: fir pine viridian olive jade apple sage emerald mint forest grass moss and verdigris. Such infinite subtleties (like a boy's moan). This morning the starlings tell me a young man plots to kill me. He is stupid and in love (and I am all envy). I will pretend to be sleeping when he comes.

The Frame Called Ruin

Fireflies are not like glass, James,
but a little spittle of green and gold, a neon snot.
No, no repeat performance necessary.

I know the need to ignite already fills you
and imagine twisting off your head—
lava spurting fiery nails, and your laughter.

*

James, can't I now call you Jim?
A secret name behind your knees
when I'm holding your hips and you are yelping?

In all the paintings we are dead.
We are all the wrong colors—
Prussian blue, Mars black, our lips

an awful brick red. We look like a war.
In death as it is in death. Our legs
tangled like grasshoppers.

End of the Line

What a relief to be dead.
To know the end of every sentence to be dead.
To know the end of every day to be dead.
To know sentences and days are an accumulation of being dead.
Relief.

I was going nowhere all along to be dead.
Take a bite out of ardor and exhaustion to be dead.
There are people falling from the trees to be dead.
And from the windows of skyscrapers.
People with lipstick, cameras, and grenades.
We all are already dead.

Get out of bed to be dead.
Eat breakfast, pee, and check e-mail to be dead.
Light a candle and talk to my dead grandmother to be dead.
Meditate to be dead.
Take medication for depression and anxiety to be dead.
Enough to kill a horse to be dead.
And wear a great dress to be dead.
A red one with white polka dots.
It's a spectator's sport to be dead.

Like the game of being drunk with friends and fortune cookies to be dead.
Not the one where you add *in bed* at the end of every fortune, but *to be dead.*
I saved fortunes in my wallet for years (with a photo of my mother and a rubber
to be dead).
The best times of your life have not yet been lived to be dead.
Trust your intuition. Your success will be great to be dead.
Friends long absent are coming back to you to be dead.
I will be dead with them.

Like Robert who died two weeks after my wedding to be dead.
And I had all these smiling pictures of him to be dead.
Or my father struggling for balance and breath as he walked me down the aisle to be dead.
Or my mother falling down the stairs and waiting alone for five hours to be dead.

Or having a heart attack for two and a half days before going to the hospital to be dead.
God, will this poem ever end?

To be dead. To be dead. To be dead.

I thought it was going to be funny to be dead.
About cookies to be dead.
I'm apparently not Zen enough to be dead.
Raised Jewish and afraid to be dead.
The Holocaust to be dead.
All things come to an end to be dead.
Insert a brilliant penultimate sentence to be dead.
Or a whisper.

Show Me Yours

The mouth is the shape
of sound, the opening
I have for you.

Shelter
of flesh and wind.

Vowels in the attic.
Valves sweat and spit.

If I whisper your name
we are close as matches
flowering pink.

*

The names you yell at night,
in the day. The names
you chew like pebbled bread.

Breakage is such sweet sorrow.

Press them hard against
the back of your teeth.

Now drumroll
as they crumble:

Tom, tom-tom,
tom, tom.

*

Can I spit you out?
Can I (safely) hold you in?

What is it like in agony,
in ecstasy. Inflections change
the sound the mouth makes.

I watched

*

for centuries, collecting teeth
on a chain. Charmed
by the various faces

of decay. Bracelet
of bone and chatter.

Everywhere I go, they follow. Chit.
Red impressions etch
the wrist.

*

Like a mother,
Let me wipe your mouth.

Like a paramour,
Let me love your mouth.

Exit becomes entrance.
Entranced by your bellows.

*

The men in their poems are incessant.
Incessant poems with Ophelia or Sabine
or Charlotte this, Charlotte that.

A gumdrop girl in your pocket
and the terrible lint of words.

How large your hunger,
how empty your mouth.

*

Poem mouth, prison mouth,
suitcase mouth, or river of milk.

Fishmouth stuffed with ovals
and a bouquet of names
gaping for air.

Mouths wear pretty ruffled heads
and drown in black water.

*

Flesh house
of arrival, of departure.

Entrance becomes exit.
Entranced by your hollows.

Wait for me on the balcony
wearing pink.

Let me lick along the gumline
as we dissipate

(last cry, last kiss).

*

When we're dying all
the loves come back.

~~Sing, no~~. Swallow
their brief return.

Skinless Love

Louise, pass the salt, please pass
        the sun—our savory mornings.

On walks with the dog I'll bring you tied like a kite to my wrist,
        your face bobbing in the moonlight.

I dream of you riding a giant spider.
        You are all dangle, darling and weightless.

Reel me in tied to your mouth (silk-spin),
        your secret glands sticky with waiting.
        Save me for later like a peppermint,
        I'll nap under your tongue, lick your furry palate.

Who needs breasts, eyebrows, or white platelets?

        I think devotion is like this:

                        skinned of art,
                a bodiless mingling.

Beyond your cotton-stuffed limbs and nylon sacks,
        your greasy cells buttered in wax.

We love beyond all these drippings,
        a love that lasts.

Notes

"Blur" is for the four lives lost on January 29, 2007 when a suicide bomber blew up a bakery in Eilat, Israel. Eilat is a popular tourist destination.

"Icarus in Love" is for Charlotte Moormon, avant-garde performance and visual artist.

"*Dawn's Wedding Feast*" from "Night, White, and Gold (for Louise Nevelson)" includes a line by Paul Éluard (*This fan with beautiful ribs*).

"Still Life (with Death)" is after Magritte's painting *The Lovers.*

"My Wife in All Things" is after André Breton's poem "Free Union."

"The Women Are Naked Again" is after Amy Morken's painting *Backwards Diving.*

"Unité d' Habitation" is after the modern, multi-family housing units designed by Le Corbusier.

"Be My Plate" includes two lines adapted from Lisa Robertson's book-length poem "The Weather" (*Sometimes I want a corset like / to harden me or garnish*).

"Fields, Ribbons, Folds: Somatic Landscapes (for Zaha Hadid)" is after four architectural works by Zaha Hadid. "*The Centre of the Body*" is after the Rosenthal Center for Contemporary Art (Cincinnati, USA); "*Vitra's Dance*" is after the Vitra Fire Station (Weil am Rhein, Germany); "*Operatic Space*" is after the Cardiff Bay Opera House (Wales, UK); and "*Soon, the Garden*" is after Landersgardenschau (Weil am Rhein, Germany).

"Abandoned Dome" is after Buckminster Fuller's geodesic dome design for homes.

"Severance" is after Amy Cutler's painting *Heiresses.*

"Two-Inch Figure Standing on an Inkwell" is after Susan Dunkerley's photograph *Waft.*

"*Black, Maroons, and White*" from "Four Reds (for Rothko)" includes a line by Wallace Stevens (*The spirit and space, the empty spirit in vacant space*).

"Construction" is in memory of the nearly 3,000 people who died on September 11, 2001 in the World Trade Center tragedy in New York City.

"Ache Becomes 'Embankment'" is after Rachel Whiteread's sculpture *Embankment* installed in the Tate London in 2005. With thanks to Zach Schomberg for the poem's final couplet.

"Fable of Flesh" is after Alberto Giacometti's sculpture *The Palace at 4 a.m.*

"I Used to Be Snow White" takes its title and first line from Mae West. The poem is after Lee Friedlander's photograph *Portland, Maine* and his photographic series *Nashville, Tennessee.*

"Crash and Burn" is after Peter Garfield's photographic series *Mobile Homes*.

"The Frame Called Ruin" is after Francis Bacon's painting *Figure in Movement, 1976*.

"End of the Line" is for my father, Moty Simcha Bar-Nadav (1940-2007).

"Skinless Love" is for the visual artists Louise Bourgeois and Louise Nevelson.

Acknowledgements

Grateful acknowledgment is made to the editors of the following publications in which these poems or versions of these poems first appeared:

AGNI, The American Poetry Review, Bellingham Review, Beloit Poetry Journal, Black Warrior Review, Blue Mesa Review, Chelsea, Cimarron Review, Colorado Review, Denver Quarterly, Fence, The Iowa Review, The Journal, The Kenyon Review, Memorious, Mid-American Review, Open City, Pebble Lake Review, Ploughshares, Poetry Daily, POOL, Prairie Schooner, TriQuarterly, and *Verse.*

Several of these poems also appeared in the chapbook *Show Me Yours* (*Laurel Review*/GreenTower Press, 2010), winner of the Midwest Poets Series Award.

With endless thanks to Bill Olsen and the wonderful staff of New Issues. With special thanks to Hilda Raz, who first helped me envision this manuscript. To Simone Muench, editor and friend supreme. To Kevin Prufer whose generous support of all things poetry continues to inspire and humble me. To Eamon Grennan who believed. To the following people whose careful reading and generous comments helped shape this book: Michelle Boisseau, Adam Clay, Rebecca Morgan Frank, John Gallaher, Leslie Adrienne Miller, Wayne Miller, and the Chicago Poetry Crew: Aaron DeLee, Sarah Jenkins, Christine Pacyk, Lana Rakhman, and Virginia Smith. To my colleagues and students at the University of Missouri-Kansas City. To The Vermont Studio Center and The Virginia Center for the Creative Arts that granted me the gifts of space, time, and community. And to Scott George Beattie whose art and life inspire me anew every day.

photo by Sharon Gottula

Hadara Bar-Nadav is the author of *A Glass of Milk to Kiss Goodnight* (*Margie*/Intuit House, 2007), which was awarded the *Margie* Book Prize. Her chapbook, *Show Me Yours* (*Laurel Review*/GreenTower Press, 2010), was awarded the Midwest Poets Series Award. She is also co-author, with Michelle Boisseau, of *Writing Poems*, 8th edition (Pearson, 2011). Her awards include fellowships from The Vermont Studio Center and The Virginia Center for the Creative Arts. She is currently an Assistant Professor of English at the University of Missouri-Kansas City and lives in Kansas City with her husband, Scott George Beattie, a furniture maker and visual artist.

The Green Rose Prize

2011: Corey Marks
The Radio Tree

2010: Seth Abramson
Northerners

2009: Malinda Markham
Having Cut the Sparrow's Heart

2008: Patty Seyburn
Hilarity

2007: Jon Pineda
The Translator's Diary

2006: Noah Eli Gordon
A Fiddle Pulled from the Throat of a Sparrow

2005: Joan Houlihan
The Mending Worm

2004: Hugh Seidman
Somebody Stand Up and Sing

2003: Christine Hume
Alaskaphrenia
Gretchen Mattox
Buddha Box

2002: Christopher Bursk
Ovid at Fifteen

2001: Ruth Ellen Kocher
When the Moon Knows You're Wandering

2000: Martha Rhodes
Perfect Disappearance